The CEO and Board Member's Survival Guide

Strategic Governance For Small to Mid-Cap
Entrepreneurial Organizations That Capitalizes on
Opportunities and Minimizes Risk

William Kraut, CPA, MBA, CITP

CGW
PUBLISHING

2015

The CEO and Board Member's Survival Guide

Strategic Governance For Small to Mid-Cap
Entrepreneurial Organizations That Capitalizes on
Opportunities and Minimizes Risk

First Edition: January 2015

ISBN 978-1-908293-34-3

CGW Publishing 2015

CGW Publishing
B1502
PO Box 15113
Birmingham
B2 2NJ
United Kingdom

www.cgwpublishing.com

mail@cgwpublishing.com

To my wonderful, loving and
always supportive wife, Marcia

Contents

Foreword...8

Introduction..10

Why You Need This Survival Guide and What It Can Do For You..10

Problems and Opportunities Facing Today's Boards of Directors...12

Who Is Bill Kraut and Why Is He Qualified to Write This Book?...13

Survival Tactics: On-the-Spot Advice for Conducting Boardroom Business...15

SECTION ONE..16

Strategy Development..18

It's Never As Simple Nor As Straightforward As Appears...19

The Astute CEO Uses His Board to Help Further Company Plans...22

The Job of the Board of Directors...........................24

The Role of Board Member Independence..............25

Mentoring the CEO..27

Board Education...28

Choosing Strategy Development Alternatives.........29

How Overly-Sophisticated Plans Miss The Mark.......30

The Differences Between Vision, Strategy and Tactics...32

Determining Value Propositions and Disseminating Them Throughout the Organization.......................34

Business Owner's Exit Strategy..............................35

SECTION TWO..38

Leadership Development...40

Developing The Company's Senior Leadership
Team...41

The Difference Between Managing Operations and
Providing Company Leadership.................................44

What Kind of Board Is Best for Your Company?........45

Selecting, Managing and Retaining Talented Board
Members...47

Finding the Best Board Member Candidates.............48

Building the Team and Assuring They Stay...............50

The Founder as Role Model...................................51

SECTION THREE...56

Board Meetings, Board Committees And Advisory
Councils...58

Running a Professional Board of Directors............59

Focusing On Corporate Governance Issues...............60

Standing and Ad Hoc Boardroom Committees..........62

Taking Advantage of Advisory Councils...................65

Differences between Boards of Directors and
Advisory Councils..67

SECTION FOUR...70

The Board's Role In Mergers And Acquisitions
(M&A)...72

Board Due Diligence...73

Factors To Consider Before Merging or Acquiring a
Company...74

Determining Synergy of the Deal and Whether It's Worthwhile..78

The M&A Playbook..**81**

Transition Planning...82

Company Due Diligence...84

Integration Planning..86

Implementation..87

Due Diligence Differences Between Selling the Business and Buying a Company.............................88

SECTION FIVE..92

Countering Cyber Risk...**94**

Risks from New Technology..................................**95**

Corporate Risk Management in An Age of Cyber Attacks..96

The Anti-Cyber Attack's Committee Charter.............98

The Critical Importance of IT Leadership...............100

APPENDIX...**104**

Job Descriptions...**106**

Sample Job Description of a Board Member Along With Some Recommendations...............................106

Contacting the Author.......................................**109**

Notes...**110**

FOREWORD

This book is intended for board directors of small, mini and micro-cap companies (public or private).

There are many sources of director education for large and mid-size companies, but very little that address the uniqueness of life in smaller company boardrooms. Growth from start-up through small cap presents unique and frequently corporate-life threatening risks along with corresponding opportunities. The board's basic responsibility is to embrace those opportunities and mitigate apparent risks.

Every board decision looms as potential for an unrecoverable situation if not handled well. Ongoing attention is paramount; the speed of disruptive change is ever increasing.

This book is not a treatise on legal or fiduciary responsibilities. It is intended to be a practical and readable guide for board directors of small, mini and micro-cap companies. Because board members of smaller companies wear more hats than their counterparts of large and mid-cap companies, they need to take care not to cross the line separating their independence from operating management.

Three major areas come to mind for board members of these smaller companies:

1. Strategy: They must be involved in the development, ongoing monitoring and tweaking of company strategy. The "annual read and approve" approach of yesterday no longer suffices.

2. Information technology governance: In today's digital environment it is crucial that smaller boards raise the issue of information technology to board level. Board leadership should adapt a wide-ranging perspective to include strategic oversight of the many areas of involvement, such as mobile applications, cloud issues, social media, disruptive present and future complexity and innovation, as well as evolving cyber security issues and regulatory issues.

3. Talent governance: Board involvement in identification, development and nurturing of the company's future leaders is of paramount importance.

This book addresses these issues and more.

Bill Kraut

INTRODUCTION

Why You Need This Survival Guide and What It Can Do For You

Let's play a game. Imagine for a moment that you could travel back in time to the sixties to attend a typical board of directors meeting of that era. Let's assume this particular board of directors' meeting you're attending was the governing body of a typical midsized company, and we'll further assume that the company was manufacturing products, since the fifties through the seventies were the heyday years of American manufacturing.

Chances are this board was composed of executives of exceptional achievements, most of them either working for the company or as retired senior executives from other companies. Board members, as a rule, have extensive experience in a variety of industries, not necessarily related to the board for which they were serving . . . and this board was no different. The common denominator was their high organizational rank and history of success.

Let's say this board, composed of twelve directors, met once every quarter, for which they were paid handsomely. The meetings invariably took place over an extended weekend at a country club or resort, and involved a few of rounds of golf, an excursion such as a day fishing and an opportunity to get better acquainted with fellow directors. Time spent on board meetings was normally kept to a minimum.

The typical conduct of a board meeting of that period was in sharp contrast to the caliber of the assembled senior executives. There was generally some halfhearted discussion surrounding items on the board's agenda but voting was essentially kept in line by the Chairman of the board (normally the company's CEO). Of course, that rubber-stamp behavior wasn't openly discussed, but the very fact that there was little if any dissension was indicative of the board Chairman's power. Sure, some of the members were in disagreement about decisions taken and grumbled about it. But, if they wanted to hold their seats and collect a generous pay package for those four quarterly meetings and if they enjoyed playing golf gratis at some of the most expensive golf courses, they kept their silence. This phenomenon was called "read and approve", and was quite common in years past.

Lawsuits brought against individual board members (as opposed to the company as an entity) happened occasionally, but only occasionally, and in each instance a team of company lawyers was sent forth to do battle against those who sought to extract easy money from the company and its board members. Lawsuits in those untroubled days were not generally a problem sitting board members had to contend with.

Problems and Opportunities Facing Today's Boards of Directors

Now return to today, the early twenty-first century and attend any board meeting. "Read and approve" is virtually a figment of the past, a pleasant memory. Today, if you sit on a board, you can rest assured that at some point or another you're going to be sued. Count on it!

Board membership is no longer a free ride. It's exacting work that takes the full attention of board members, who must at all times be aware of their duties and responsibilities to the shareholders as well as laws established by state, local and federal regulators (more often than not, a confusing array of legislated requirements). If they're not, they're likely to fall prey to stockholder lawsuits or, in extreme cases, face arrest. You can reasonably conclude that sitting board members have the obligation to assure they're protected by company indemnification and by directors' and officers' liability insurance.

Board members in the twenty-first century deal with an extensive set of complicated issues including strategy development, disruptive technologies, fast changing- social, political and economic environments, mergers and acquisitions, corporate finance complexities, cyber risk and an entire spectrum of related issues that cannot be skimmed over. Due diligence is an absolute requirement. The board member who rubber stamps the Chairman's wishes rather than exhaustively analyzing how they affect stockholder value is a board member headed for trouble. Need I mention Enron, Tyco, WorldCom, or Health South?

This book is devoted to help you—the board member of an entrepreneurial small to mid cap company—understand what you must do to survive and flourish in this demanding environment. It also contains a special section describing cyber threats in the boardroom and what board members need to do to protect themselves (Section Five).

The subtitle of this book says it all: Strategic Governance For Small-to-Mid-Cap Entrepreneurial Organizations That Capitalizes on Opportunities and Minimizes Risk.

Who Is Bill Kraut and Why Is He Qualified to Write This Book?

I'm an accomplished, board-savvy advisor on strategic and financial issues to firms ranging from start-ups to mature private and public companies. I've had a distinguished 30+ year career as a CPA and Chartered Global Management Accountant and Certified Information Technology Professional (CITP) with Amper, Politziner & Mattia LLP (now EisnerAmper, LLP), one of the largest New York area CPA firms. I served in a number of leadership roles including managing partner of audit/SEC services and chief information officer.

My advisory experience on board strategy covers a wide range of board issues from long-term capital planning to crisis-related tactics. I'm a respected expert on risk management, fraud risk, audit committee responsibilities and regulatory compliance. My record of accomplishment includes helping clients with business strategy development, operational improvement, organizational change, human capital development, IPO preparation, sale-preparation, and negotiation strategies, due diligence, as well as exit strategy development.

I've worked with the boards of directors of high tech, biotech, pharmaceutical, communications, media, internet, service and light manufacturing companies. I am currently the lead independent director and audit committee chair of a NYSE company and a board member and audit committee chair of the New Jersey Chapter of the National Association of Corporate Directors. I am currently a partner with Newport Board Group LLC, a consulting firm that specializes in advising CEOs and board members. My expertise involves showing companies with rapid growth issues how to survive and flourish when they find themselves in the predicament of being "too big to be small and too small to be big."[1]

Finally, in addition to all of my practical business experience, I'm a National Association of Corporate Directors (NACD) Governance Fellow, I hold a MBA, and I'm an Adjunct Professor at Monmouth University Graduate School and a Mentor-In-Residence at the Rothman Institute of Entrepreneurship, Fairleigh Dickinson University.

Survival Tactics: On-the-Spot Advice for Conducting Boardroom Business

This book is a policy guide meant for veteran board members, new board members, and those executives interested in joining boards. It identifies areas of concern for CEOs as board members as well as other board members and suggests principles for conducting board business. As such it doesn't get into detailed descriptions of supporting procedures. That's best left to company accountants and lawyers.

Instead, what readers will take away from each section is practical, down-to-earth policy advice that, if handled properly, will help avoid the pitfalls of board membership and fulfill their legal and fiduciary obligations to the shareholders.

To help achieve that end, readers will see text boxes throughout the book, like the one shown below, summarizing key points. These boxes are titled Survival Tactics, because they're focused on helping board members conduct their boardroom affairs and avoid unnecessary risk. Consider these as complementary advice that adds to the policy suggestions described in the individual sections and chapters. Here is the first:

> Do not consider a board membership
> unless you are willing to accept due
> diligence as a way of life.

SECTION ONE

STRATEGY DEVELOPMENT

"A strategy is something like, an innovative new product; globalization, taking your products around the world; be the low-cost producer. A strategy is something you can touch; you can motivate people with; be number one and number two in every business. You can energize people around the message."

Jack Welch, Retired CEO and Chairman of the Board, General Electric

"What we need to do is always lean into the future; when the world changes around you and when it changes against you—what used to be a tail wind is now a head wind—you have to lean into that and figure out what to do because complaining isn't a strategy."

Jeff Bezos, Founder, CEO and Chairman of the Board, Amazon.com

"Capital isn't scarce. Vision is."

Sam Walton, CEO of Wal-Mart

IT'S NEVER AS SIMPLE NOR AS STRAIGHTFORWARD AS APPEARS

This segment describes what happens when the company CEO confuses his role of strategist and planner with that of operating executive. Over the years a body of principles and practices has evolved that clearly illustrates the folly of the company CEO trying to do both.

Oversight vs. execution is a concept that appears easy to understand. On paper or on a computer screen you wonder how it could be misunderstood, and some might even wonder why I'm bringing it up. But management theory is just one side of the coin. Like every theory on which management practices are based, reality can be anything but.

The way things work in actual practice is often messy as Jonathan discovered:

The first board of directors on which I served was engaged in pharmaceutical manufacturing. The company had recently been involved in an expensive product recall. Because of the company's problems, the CEO, a scientist himself, was frustrated by his chief operating officer's inability to resolve the problem. Anxious to provide a fast fix, the CEO clearly stepped over the line into operations by taking control and imposing tightened quality practices in manufacturing.

Control is good up to a point. The problem starts when the CEO departs from his role as chief strategist for the company and Chairman (or member) of the board and meddles with operations. Unfortunately, the more a CEO digs into operating details himself the greater the possibility of confusion.

The CEO's overreach shut off much of new product development as he took personal responsibility for reassigning scientists and engineers to resolve what turned out to be deep procedural quality problems. The absence of those technical professionals from their primary job of new product development took its toll as the company lagged behind in bringing an important new product to market. Its main competitors leaped on the mistake and introduced similar products and took business away from the company. The company had to play an expensive game of catch-up. Results: The company lost money for the quarter.

> The essence of the CEO's job is strategy, not tactics; plan, not do; policy, not implementation.

The Society for Human Resource Management put it as plainly as it gets: "The President (CEO) is responsible for providing strategic leadership for the company by working with the board and other management to establish long-range goals, strategies, plans, and policies."[2]

Joel Trammell, CEO of Khorus, claims these overarching responsibilities for chief executive officers as reported in Entrepreneur Magazine:

Own the vision. A CEO should determine and communicate the organization's strategic direction.

Provide the proper resources. Only the CEO can perform the task of balancing resources, the two most important ones being capital and people.

Build the culture. Culture is the set of shared attitudes, goals, behaviors and values that characterize a group.

Make good decisions.

Oversee and deliver the company's expected performance. (This is the area that's often hard to define and causes the most trouble when the CEO fails to make a distinction between planning and execution.)

The CEO also serves as the interface between internal operations and external stakeholders (in his role reporting to the board of directors).[3]

Effectiveness vs. Efficiency

Another way to describe the difference between planning and execution is by defining the difference between effectiveness and efficiency. Succinctly, effectiveness is doing the right things; efficiency is doing things right. The CEO's job falls smack on the side of effectiveness, doing the right things. His involvement in efficiency is indirect, since he rightfully expects his operating lieutenants to handle the organization's efficiency, doing things right.

> The CEO's job is doing the right things. The Chief Operating Officer's job is doing things right. Trouble starts when the CEO tries to do both.

The Astute CEO Uses His Board to Help Further Company Plans

Mike Myatt, CEO of N2Growth explains the relationship between the CEO and the company's board of directors: "I've yet to meet a CEO who at some point in time hasn't been frustrated by their board—it goes with the territory. That said, it should be the exception, and not the rule. Ultimately, chief executives deserve the board relationships they develop. As a CEO, your board can be one of your greatest allies. Conversely, and just as easily, they can be a significant contributor to your undoing resulting in an early and unnecessary demise."[4]

The key words to take away from Myatt's comments are: ". . . chief executives deserve the board relationships they develop." Never have truer words been spoken. Anybody who subscribes to business periodicals such as The Wall Street Journal or Bloomberg Businessweek has undoubtedly read numerous examples of boards of directors who have revolted against their chief executives officers and deposed them. Which argues the case that astute CEOs should take full advantage of the many talents of their boards to help them further company plans. This teamwork will keep the CEO and board members reading from the same page, and will avert many communication problems.

As reported in an article, "Essential Elements of an Effective CEO-Board relationship," written in Russell Reynolds Associates' Board Magazine, the CEO should "proactively seek board input outside of board meetings: Outside of board meetings, with the knowledge of the Chairman, the CEO actively and informally seeks board members' informal input, feedback and guidance on strategy. When the CEO presents strategies for approval, he/she is able to predict (and acknowledge) likely areas of disagreement with individual board members."[5]

Private and individual discussions with board members outside of board meetings allow the CEO to establish a mutual understanding of the issues with board members, expose trouble areas and gain board members' cooperation. These discussions often unearth hidden problems in time to resolve them and reshape issues before they're presented in the formal atmosphere of the boardroom.

Reaching agreements with board members outside and before board meetings is key to successful board meetings.

THE JOB OF THE BOARD OF DIRECTORS

Mark, a successful entrepreneur who had started three software companies, built them into multi-million-dollar businesses and sold them for a tidy profit, served on the boards of four different companies. Over the years he had observed that board members are sometimes led astray by their chairmen's forceful personalities.

"One of the boards I served on was in the online game business and wanted to diversify by entering the software game market. Neither the board members nor the CEO and his senior staff had any experience in making, selling or distributing software products. So they asked me for advice, which I freely gave.

Unfortunately, the Chairman's request didn't stop there. The company acquired a company that produced accounting software. Although I had established a board committee to oversee transitioning the new business, the Chairman (and CEO) asked me to work directly with the operating departments on the integration process.

This went beyond the charter of my oversight responsibilities as a board director, and could have materially interfered with my objective judgment of whether or not the acquired business was capable of meeting company goals, and whether or not the general manager of the newly acquired company could handle the transition to the game business. That would have amounted to abandoning my primary responsibility to the shareholders. I dug in my heels. It's never a good idea for a board member to get personally involved executing policy, so I declined. The Chairman and I had a face-to-face meeting where I explained my reservations. It wasn't long after that the Chairman came to his senses and withdrew his request."

> Board members should keep in mind the phrase "arms length" as a guide to their relationship with operating departments.

The Role of Board Member Independence

Board members everywhere have the obligation to recognize their basic responsibilities regarding corporate governance, accounting to the shareholders, fiduciary roles (such as assuring adequate financial resources, approving dividends and reviewing merger & acquisitions), strategy review, approval of new corporate policies, annual budget approval, and CEO issues such as selection, retention, performance review, compensation and succession.

But, like CEOs, directors often lose sight of the fine line that separates oversight and execution. On occasion, as in the example cited above, board members submerge themselves by taking charge of some aspect of operations. That's sometimes because they've had the same experiences elsewhere and are itching to help and display their competence. More often than not, it's because of pressure from the public, shareholders or government agencies for further accountability those outside groups consider lacking. When that's an issue, chances are it's going to be in the areas of fiduciary responsibility or corporate governance.

There's an entire spectrum of potential problem areas facing board members, including:

- An overpowering Chairman of the board dictating policy (not as frequent anymore, but still around).

- Institutional loyalty: Pressure from company or family members (major shareholders) to adopt a specific point of view.

- Conflicts of interest arising from serving on the board of one company but owning stock in a competitor's company.

- Directors so highly specialized that their contribution to their boards is narrow and restricted and they are unable to grasp the essentials of strategy.

Harry Edelson, managing partner of Edelson Technology Partners writing for Boards & Directors, describes a litany of dysfunctional behavior he has found in small-company boards. He concludes that "very few boards are so good that they could not be improved. A useful topic for discussion once a year at board meetings should be: 'What can be done to improve the meetings?' If you want to accomplish something at a board meeting, do the work in conjunction with other members beforehand. The board of directors will function best if it is prepared, not surprised."[6]

Probably the best advice a company's board of directors can take away from this is to invest the time and money to get professional consulting help to structure the board and establish its governing procedures. The smaller the company and newer the board the more this help is needed.

Mentoring the CEO

As the saying goes in business, "It's lonely at the top." Anybody who has held the top post understands the top executive's feeling of isolation. Under those circumstances, it's easy for company CEOs to lose perspective, especially since they make decisions that can spell life or death for the company. They, like everybody, else need help, if for nothing more than to gain a fresh perspective.

CEOs need measured degrees of mentoring. Obviously, the less experienced the CEO, the more mentoring needed. But even seasoned CEOs need the reassurance that comes from receiving advice from their board members — presumably, all of them seasoned veterans in their own right. The Chairman of the board, in particular, can be helpful, assuming the CEO and Chairman are two different persons.

There are also peer groups that CEOs can go to for help and advice, such as the CEO Roundtable.

Local Chambers of Commerce know the groups in their area best suited to senior executives and board members. Some colleges also sponsor incubators where CEOs can make valuable contacts. All of these groups are worthwhile, and particularly suitable for CEOs and board members of small or start-up companies. CEOs often use executive coaches to fulfill this function.

Board Education

The National Association of Corporate Directors (NACD) has these words emblazoned on its home page: "No One Should underestimate directors' need for continuing education."[7] The NACD excels in providing such education to its members. I would encourage every board member to take advantage by joining this fine organization. It pays dividends in knowledge and contacts.

Your membership also puts you in touch with thousands of board members across the country, many in your area – an invaluable source of information. Many have, or are facing, the same problems you have; it's a chance to exchange ideas that may help you resolve problems or spark an idea for new opportunities.

> Never underestimate the value of both mentoring and continuing education. They provide you with the opportunity to elevate your performance as a board member.

CHOOSING STRATEGY DEVELOPMENT ALTERNATIVES

Over the span of her career, Janet, an accomplished senior executive in the fashion industry, sat on a dozen boards, most of those boards effective, a couple not so. She tells this experience about a not-so-effective board that turned into an effective one with the appointment of a new Chairman of the board and CEO:

The company was an upscale mid-cap regional retailer in men's and women's haute couture clothing . . . with a twist. The twist was exceptional courtier service with private viewing and dressing rooms complete with wine and cheese service that made its customers feel like royalty (at a price).

When I joined the board, the company had stores in six large metropolitan areas across the South and what turned out to be ambitious plans for 15 more across the USA. It had been a fast growth startup run by an entrepreneur who had given birth to five other companies and later sold them (not an unusual situation). But like some entrepreneurs who were great at startups, this CEO wasn't adept at managing the business. His job as he saw it was to run as fast as he could opening new stores while keeping his fingers crossed that his senior executives could keep up with him.

At this crucial juncture of the company's business, the COO with his boss' permission hired a technical consulting firm to install sophisticated information systems to control costs, inventories, purchasing and distribution. That moved proved disastrous. The systems were so complicated it took a dozen Philadelphia lawyers to understand them. Within six months management removed the new systems and the company faced bankruptcy from a combination of excess costs and playing musical chairs with its essential systems. The board replaced the CEO who managed, with the aid of an infusion of capital and commonsense, to rescue the company.

How Overly-Sophisticated Plans Miss The Mark

Strategy is not esoteric; it means choosing among alternatives. When you decide which customer to cater to and which ones not to—that is a strategic decision.

Ongoing involvement of the board with strategy development is important, not just an annual review, approve, then go play golf. The duty of board members is to challenge management's assumptions, both stated and presumed. Nothing ever stays the same and presumptive suppositions can frequently be in error. The disruptive economic, geopolitical and technological environment of today is here to stay.

Edward L. Cochran of the Honeywell Technology Center examined system failures and arrived at this conclusion: " . . . the complexity of the systems involved combined with the communications requirements . . . led to performance demands that individual humans are fundamentally not capable of sustaining."[8]

Gurdeep Mahal, writing in an article for Quality Digest listed four reasons why complex systems (in this case, quality systems) fail: Inadequate resources, lack of clarity around program ownership and roles, developing a system that's too complicated, and lack of management engagement. [9]

When it comes to systems needed for reporting and control, the best advice is to install the simplest systems that will do the job. Keep the mantra of "simpler is better" as the company's guideline. Simple systems are easier to understand and easier to operate. If you're upgrading from a manual system to a computer system, run both side by side until you work out the bugs in the computer system. As in football, you've got to master running and blocking before you start the passing game. It's attention to fundamentals that count, and it's lack of attention to fundamentals that get a company in trouble.

> Sophisticated systems may be the 'newest thing on the block,' but until they're tested stay with what you know is workable.

The Differences Between Vision, Strategy and Tactics

Vision is what the founder or company's board want the company to be. For example, the largest optometry chain in the Northwest, 100% guaranteed overnight delivery service and the lowest price on the market.

Leslie Kossoff, management consultant and author of the book, Executive Thinking: The Dream, The Vision, The Mission Achieved explains vision. "We have such beautiful pictures in our heads about what we believe could be. . . The executive has a comprehensive picture in his or her head, usually without specific words to describe it. Also, the dream is iterative. As the executive learns and experiences more, and as aspects of the dream are manifest the dream becomes better and more clearly defined."[10]

A statement of the company's vision, sometimes termed a mission statement, needs to be burnished in every employee's mind so front-line employees through the Chairman and CEO are well aware of where the company wants to be.

As Yogi Berra famously said, "If you don't know where you're going you might not get there." Don't allow that kind of uncertainty to reign in your company.

Strategy, on the other hand, as Michael Porter, strategy guru, defines it, is ". . . about being different. It means answering the question 'What are we trying to accomplish?'"[11] Strategy, in other words, is how a company intends to achieve its vision. If its vision is to become the largest optometry chain in the Northwest, the company must decide if it wants to buy-up mom and pop optometry stores or build an optometry empire through expansion.

Vision and strategy are the province of the CEO and board of directors.

Tactics, on the other hand, is the job of the operating arm of the organization. Its job is to carry out the company's strategy. Tactics should always be expressed as specific actions, accompanied by budgeted costs and timetables and assignment of individual employees responsible for completing the actions. Anything less may threaten successful completion of the company's strategy.

Strategy is, by definition, long term. It may take years to become the largest optometry dealer in the Northwest. Tactics is always short term, and articulates the many steps it takes year by year to achieve the company's strategy. Tactics may change. For example, if the company's strategy is to expand from within, it may still decide at some point to buyout some existing mom and pop stores. That change is tactical.

Determining Value Propositions and Disseminating Them Throughout the Organization

The next step in the process is creating value propositions that clearly and succinctly express the value the company brings to its customers as articulated in its vision. For example, if the company is in the optometry business, a typical value proposition might be "We have the cheapest prices in the Pacific Northwest. If you find cheaper we'll pay you the difference." (That's one of the reasons Walmart is so successful.) Or another value proposition: "We guarantee our eyeglasses for however long you own them. If you ever have a problem, return them, no questions asked. Period!" Or "One hour service or no charge for your examination."

Your value proposition can't be vague, wishy-washy. "Our products are the best in the business" doesn't tell you anything. Neither does "Our services provided fast." That's meaningless because fast could mean anything.

And be sure that the board of directors as well as every employee in the company is on board. If an optometry shop—just a single one—falls down by not meeting the value proposition, the word will get out and the company's reputation damaged. It's the CEO's duty to keep the company's value proposition fresh in everybody's mind and foremost in their thoughts. It can be enlightening, from time to time, to verify directly from your customers how they see your value proposition. The variances you encounter are frequently astonishing. Over time the company's adherence to value propositions can drift. You can prevent that by constantly reiterating the value proposition message.

> Consider the company's value proposition a "must adhere to" requirement. And test adherence at random intervals. Otherwise it will slip over time. People have short memories.

Business Owner's Exit Strategy

What happens to the business when the company owner or chief executive dies or retires or sells the business (to outside parties, employees or their children)? Those questions need to be answered when the owner starts the business and updated annually to account for changes over time such as the (hopefully) increasing value of the business.

The exit strategy should answer such questions as succession, the board member responsible for handling the transition, how the exit strategy plan is documented and specific instructions regarding who now owns what and how much.

Regrettably, too often the question of succession is answered under emergency circumstances when the owner dies or is involved in a debilitating accident or a financial crisis erupts. Decisions taken in an emergency under pressure may be poor decisions. Maximizing valuation can rarely be achieved without a plan. Some of the worst valuations I have seen during sales of the business have been when a spouse is forced to sell the company to pay estate taxes, or because the spouse was not involved in company operations and was therefore unaware of what the company's true value was.

An effective exit strategy is really two plans. The first assumes everything will go as planned; the second assumes it won't. In other words, contingency planning. Both are needed. And both call for the attention of an accountant and lawyer.

Regarding exit strategy, Jennifer Lawton, owner of library chain Just Books, Inc. said, "I began to see my exit strategy less as a termination, and more as a logical part of the high goals I had set for both my company and myself. I may pursue an acquisition, take the company public, merge with another concern, methodically increase sales to a higher level, or shoot for rapid 200 percent growth. In achieving any of these goals, I will have, in fact, 'exited.' My company will have moved from one phase to the next, its 'exit' from one level becoming its 'entrance' to the next. The reality is that unless you define that end or change, your business may change in a way that wasn't in your plan."[12]

SECTION TWO

LEADERSHIP DEVELOPMENT

"I'm responsible for this company. I stand behind the results. I know the details, and I think the CEO has to be the moral leader of the company. I think high standards are good, but let's not anybody be confused, it's about performance with integrity. That's what you have to do."

Jeffrey Immelt, CEO of General Electric

"Leaders get out in front and stay there by raising the standards by which they judge themselves – and by which they are willing to be judged."

Fred Smith, CEO of FedEx

"The greatest leader is not necessarily the one who does the greatest things. He is the one that gets the people to do the greatest things."

Ronald Reagan, 40th President of the United States

Sometimes, I think my most important job as a CEO is to listen for bad news. If you don't act on it, your people will eventually stop bringing bad news to your attention and that is the beginning of the end."

Bill Gates, Former Chairman and CEO of Microsoft

DEVELOPING THE COMPANY'S SENIOR LEADERSHIP TEAM

McKinsey consultants got it right when they wrote "No one would dispute that top teams are critical to an organization's success, yet few top teams feel they get it right. Poor team performance breeds silos, competing agendas, turf wars, and indecision; high performance produces organizational coherence and focus."[13]

John Hall, CEO of Influence & Company, a company that assists individuals and brands in growing their influence through thought leadership and content marketing programs, suggests basic steps a leader can take to develop a phenomenal team. It's interesting to apply a few of Hall's points to the development of senior leadership:

- Insist on the best. Never settle for mediocre people or mediocre performance. At the senior level every leader should have already been vetted to assure top level performance. With internal hires that's easy to do because their performance is always under the microscope. Hiring from outside is another matter. Thorough vetting is required to avoid a mistake.

- Play to your leaders' strengths. Gangbuster operating heads, such as production managers are different persons than introspective engineering design managers.

41

Each operates in a different way and in a different environment. Placing one in the job of the other simply won't cut it. They'll both be unhappy and produce substandard work.

- Develop processes around your successful practices that mimic them. Create guidelines and checklists that specify every step. For example, in the hiring process, develop a standard list of the type of questions that expose strengths and weaknesses of job candidates.

- Invest time and money for leaders so they can apply what they've learned to those who follow them. This step is complementary to the processes just mentioned but it places those processes in the hands of leaders best able to apply them.

Mary Genis, Executive Director, the Tyra Banks TZONE Foundation and Owner of Sintra Consulting describes why so many leadership efforts fall short: "Helping managers become visionary leaders is possible, but it is not easy. Knowing what to do is different from knowing how to do it, and this is certainly the case for developing leadership effectiveness. Leaders learn about leadership by being in a certain mindset. They become stronger leaders by learning from past experiences, and becoming wiser predictors of changing circumstances. Leaders learn how to develop followers by carefully planning and executing actions that build support, enthusiasm and confidence from a wide range of stakeholders. These are not activities that occur in a classroom; they happen on the job."[14]

Genis recommends leadership programs that include:

1. Designing a structure that yields time for self-reflection and builds self-awareness.

2. Requiring individualized learning objectives and self-development plans.

3. Differentiating between good and great performance.

4. Allowing growth and development to occur in real time, while on the job.

It's apparent that leadership development is both the aim and necessity of the organization. Because of the difficulty achieving both, your best bet is to tailor-make your leadership program and have it endorsed by leaders throughout the organization.

The Difference Between Managing Operations and Providing Company Leadership

It's easy sometimes to be unsure about distinctions between managing and leading. This is particularly true when comparing the functions of the board of directors and the company's operating departments. The following chart should clear up some of the confusion.

Table Comparing Leading (Board of Directors) vs. Managing (Operations)

Board of Directors	Operating Department
Assures mission of company is maintained.	Carries out mission of company.
Decides where to invest capital.	Achieves best return on investment.
As company's thought leaders, establishes vision and strategy.	Tactical, action arm of the company. Makes the products and delivers the services.
Does the right things.	Does things right.
Effective.	Efficient.
Creates the means.	Provides the structure.
Prepares company to meet new challenges.	Implements procedures for new challenges.

Acquires companies.	Merges operations.
Long range view.	Short range outlook.
Asks what and why.	Determines when and where.
Challenges status quo.	Follows established methods and procedures.
Envisions the future	Administers the present.
Examines possibilities.	Handles details of the here and now.
Imagines the possible.	Deals with the probable.

What Kind of Board Is Best for Your Company?

There are a few different types of boards for small to mid-cap companies.. Listed below are three of the most popular:

The most frequent, especially for small companies or startups, is a working board. Board members roll up their sleeves, take an active role on the board, attend all board meetings, chair committees (both standing and ad hoc), and do their share of the work. In a truly working board such as this, synergy $(1+1=3)$ rules.

A popular approach for mid-cap companies is using an industry board. It's composed of successful executives recruited from companies within the same industry. The value of a board like this, especially in a period of rapid company growth, is the experience board members bring to the table. These contributors are in the best position to help their companies capitalize on opportunities and avoid pitfalls.

Other types of boards include functional boards with specialists such as CPAs, lawyers, information technology professionals and/or investment bankers, depending on company needs. There are also boards composed of high profile nationally recognized business leaders, or boards with high profile community leaders.

Many boards are hybrid combinations of the types discussed above.

> The type of board a company uses at different stages of its development is crucial to company success. The board constituency should change over time to reflect the needs of the company as it grows and expands.

SELECTING, MANAGING AND RETAINING TALENTED BOARD MEMBERS

According to Barry M. Weinman, "A good Board can't make a company, but a bad one will inevitably kill it." He should know. As managing director and co-founding partner emeritus, of Allegis Capital he has worked with dozens of boards, both good and bad, and he knows what works and what doesn't.

Michelle Zatlyn, co-founder of Cloudfare, agrees that hiring wrong people can severely damage a company. "When we hire . . . I ask about a project, product, or time when the potential hire had to start something and end it over a period of weeks or a couple of months. Some people can rattle off lots of examples, and some people can't. It becomes clear who is biased toward action."[15] As Zatlyn's comments imply, you want board members who will roll up their sleeves and contribute, not board members who just collect their board fees and exploit the publicity of their board positions.

Finding the Best Board Member Candidates

Use these guiding principles to select board members that meet your company's criteria for corporate governance:

First determine what your company's priorities will be for the next several years. Then select seasoned professionals who can help you achieve those priorities. If, for example, you're building an online mail order business reach out to professionals that have in-depth know-how from companies such as Amazon.com or eBay.

For your mail order business, select board members with complementary experience in law, finance, distribution, and marketing. Their combination perspective will help you spot problems and opportunities that a less diverse board won't be able to. The lawyer will make sure the board is in compliance with governmental regulations. If you need connections to seek funding select a banker, investment banker or private investor.

Don't select board members in a vacuum. You need to make sure their personalities mesh. If, for example, you select two board members who have a history of conflict or board members with nasty dispositions you'll get board members choosing up sides and fighting, while the more important goal of company success is sidetracked. You may also find excessively aggressive members pushing an agenda far beyond the ability of the company's resources.

In general, for small to mid-cap companies a small board may be preferable to a larger board. The larger the board the harder it is to get them all together at the same time. And the larger the board the greater the possibility for disagreements overwhelming accomplishment of the agenda.

Social networking, global e-commerce and online retail sales are a growing force and represent many new avenues of opportunities for companies. It's not uncommon nowadays for boards to have at least one of its members thoroughly familiar with both the technical and business sides of cyberspace. Recognition of its importance extends to cyber protection for board members and their companies.

> The selection of talented board members in a time of rapid economic change and increased government regulation becomes critically important. The days when CEOs and company chairmen selected directors on the basis of who will be easier to manipulate is no longer viable.

Building the Team and Assuring They Stay

Robert Finocchio, venture partner with Advanced Technology Partners, and former Chairman of the board of Informix Corporation, suggests several rules for a board Chairman managing the board of directors. Following these rules will build a solid team of board members and assure their retention. Among them are:

Manage the company well and demonstrate to board members how it is done. Board members respect a board Chairman who is successful and will emulate him or her.

Foster an innovative culture. Welcome the discussion of new ideas, accept the ones that will be beneficial to the company, and never ridicule any idea a board member proposes. Encourage board members to make suggestions.

Don't forget that communication is key. Board members in the dark make bad decisions. Communicate formally, informally, in board meetings and in private meetings away from the board, collectively and individually.

Encourage full and open access between board members and the company's senior executives for information exchange. Informed board members make better decisions.

Control the agenda, pace and time of board meetings. Be direct and a step ahead of board members. Don't pussyfoot around. Drive to the heart of matters and reach concrete decisions.

Some overly aggressive board chairmen make the mistake of positioning themselves against the board. Do that and make no mistake about it: you lose. Worst of all, it encourages board members to arrive at decisions independently instead of cohesively. Therein lies anarchy.

Human nature tells you that board members will make bizarre decisions from time to time. Not often, but in every case push back. Never put yourself in the position of acknowledging or endorsing decisions that don't make sense. The board members will respect you for it.

Build a special relationship with one or two board members; alliances with board members you can rely on for unwavering support when crucial issues are on the line.

Measure performance and decisions with reliable metrics. Every major decision the board makes should always be measureable in dollars and cents as well as operational performance indicators.

The Founder as Role Model

Minerva, the Roman goddess of wisdom, is said to have sprung full-blown from the forehead of Zeus. Similarly, an organization's culture begins life in the head of its founder, springing from the founder's ideas about truth, reality, and the way the world works." So begins an abstract The Role of the Founder in Creating Organizational Culture by Edgar H. Schein, Sloan Fellows Professor of Management at the Sloan School of Management, Massachusetts Institute of Technology, Cambridge.

Think Steve Jobs, Bill Gates, Sam Walton, Jeff Bezos and you get the idea. As company founders, true entrepreneurs, they knew the secret to starting new businesses and growing them into giant American companies.

So it's natural to assume that companies should establish scalable patterns that promising leaders in the organization can use to climb the corporate ladder themselves. And doesn't it also make sense to have board members pattern their performance based on the founder as role model, assuming he or she has been successful?

These scalable patterns are often difficult to express in metrics. For example, Apple's annual revenue is over 182 billion. How can that be scaled down to a district sales manager? Sure, anything's possible, but you need to make several assumptions; otherwise you're comparing apples to oranges (excuse the pun).

Kevin Sharer, former CEO of Amgen and currently a senior lecturer at Harvard Business School, says this about capturing the best leadership behavior to use for role models: "We had to put the focus on the behaviors we expected leaders to display, and those had to be spelled out by a top team that was highly engaged, intellectually and emotionally, in the process.[16] In other words, not an easy-to-define characteristic

set. Some thought has to be put into selecting role
model behavior.

Here are a few of those behavior characteristics
that some board chairmen have used to determine
role model behavior:

Probably the most important characteristic is a
commitment to help newer board members get
their "sea legs." It helps to have each new member
assigned to a veteran board member who will
provide the necessary early guidance.

Needless to say this veteran board member
doing the mentoring should have a strong work
ethic and a penchant for getting things done.

Integrity means everything. In terms of board
service it means not accepting second-rate
solutions to problems, not skipping over one
agenda item to work on something easier, and
refusing to compromise on issues that either make
no sense or will cause the board and company
harm.

Have well-honed decision-making skills. This is
one area in particular that new board members can
zero in on by asking themselves what decisions the
role model made, and those he or she avoided. The
new member can go to school especially on the
decisions not made.

The role model will accept personal
responsibility for his actions. He or she will not shy

away from facing unpleasant truths. Nothing communicates decisiveness and courage more.

Being open to innovation, cultural shifts, and accepting the inevitability of forward progress is another key requisite.

> Top notch role models are a crucial element contributing to the success of new board members. In fact, they're priceless.

SECTION THREE

BOARD MEETINGS, BOARD COMMITTEES AND ADVISORY COUNCILS

"It takes 20 years to build a reputation and five minutes to ruin it. If you think about that, you'll do things differently."

Warren Buffett, CEO of Berkshire Hathaway

"The world is changing very fast. Big will not beat small anymore. It will be the fast beating the slow."

Rupert Murdoch, CEO of 21st Century Fox

"It's in our best interest to put some of the old rules aside and create new ones and follow the consumer—what the consumer wants and where the consumer wants to go."

Robert Iger, CEO of The Walt Disney Company

"When you innovate, you've got to be prepared for everyone telling you you're nuts."

Larry Ellison, CEO of Oracle

RUNNING A PROFESSIONAL BOARD OF DIRECTORS

I don't think anybody who has held a seat on a board of directors will forget the beating company boards took as a result of debacles caused by public failings such as Arthur Andersen (at one time arguably the most prestigious public accounting firm in the country), and white collar criminals such as Bernie Madoff. The result: increased federal regulation, tougher prosecutors and increased fines and penalties.

Today board membership is different. For one thing there are many more independent directors, more vigilant oversight from board Chairman and lead board members, greater disclosure of the names of directors and what they're paid, audit committees composed entirely of independent directors, and other improvements. And, I might add, more and more boards are taking steps independent of federal regulation to assure honest and straightforward exposure of board transactions.

Those changes have ushered in a new era of corporate governance but they don't address what happens when the board members officially meet and the boardroom doors are shut. And they certainly don't reveal how boards organize their deliberations.

> Unquestionably, today's board members are more informed than board members of generations past. In today's challenging environment board members must become familiar with a host of requirements and regulations to perform their jobs to expectations.

Focusing On Corporate Governance Issues

Josh Linkner, CEO and Managing Partner of Detroit Venture Partners, serial-entrepreneur and founder and former Chairman and CEO of ePrize (the largest interactive promotion agency in the world), suggests key steps board chairmen can take to assure that boards focus on the right corporate governance issues at the right time and in the right manner to arrive at high quality decisions that meet the spirit of the law and their requirements to shareholders.[17] Among them are:

Provide board members the opportunity to review the proposed board agenda for the next meeting well ahead of the meeting so they can thoughtfully consider the issues before them.

On key or controversial items on the agenda, discuss them individually with selected board members so the Chairman is not hit with a barrage of questions and objections during the board meeting.

For each required agenda item, assign action items to responsible board members. Have a member keep notes of actions assigned, board members responsible for each and every action, timetables for completion of assignments, reporting procedures and metrics that will be used to measure results of actions taken.

Despite the pressure associated with making decisions affecting the company's bottom line and the lives of company employees—or more probably, because of those pressures—don't rush to judgment. Stay poised and focused at all times. Get as much information as possible for each and every planned board action before the action is taken. Rational decisions seldom result when board actions are taken in the heat of the moment.

Many companies today are also establishing more formalized procedures to determine and regulate the board's agenda, such as:

Drafting boardroom conventions that define the responsibilities of board members and limit their decision-making authority both in the general board meetings and in committee.

Defining those company-wide decisions that board members best handle and company-wide decisions best taken by the company's executives. This means that the company CEO must wear two hats and be able to distinguish which hat to wear at which time.

Developing a set of rules that define specifically what those decisions are. These can range over literally dozens of subjects such as governance, finance, competitive studies, risk management, capital budget, compliance and a host of other subjects.

Writing an annual schedule for board discussion of subjects crucial to the company's success and times of the year that committees meet. This keeps all board members focused on key issues and helps them prepare for board discussions.

> The range and complexity of corporate governance subjects demands procedural assistance, some of which are specified by law. It's imperative that board members know and follow those procedures.

Standing and Ad Hoc Boardroom Committees

According to a report issued by Tapestry Networks Audit Committee Leadership Network in North America, 70 percent of S&P 500 companies have four standing committees, and 14 percent have six or more standing committees.

Standing committees vary from company to company, but many have an audit committee, compensation & management development committee, corporate governance and nominating committee.

What follows is a representative list of standing or ad hoc (formed for a special purpose) committees and a description of the subjects they cover. This is not an inclusive list. Other committees can be formed to address the company's needs. Some of the committees listed below may also be ad hoc.

Committee	Purpose
Governance	Oversees board education, rules of governance, self-assessment and management of board.
Audit	Audits reliability of company's financial statements and related internal controls, selects and oversees outside auditor and assures compliance with legal and regulatory requirements. Oversees finance committee (and sometimes take its place), and when appropriate oversees internal audit function.
Nominations	Selects of new board members, their orientation and identification of needed board member skills. (Sometimes overlaps or combines with governance committee.)

Executive	Oversees the CEO, hires the new CEO and acts on behalf of the board between meetings when required.
Finance	Oversees preparation of annual budget, approval of capital expenditures and quarterly review of budget variances. Reviews key profit indicators (KPI). Also called budget committee.
Fundraising	Develops, implements and follows-up on solicitation of funds from outside sources.
Bylaws	Synchronizes company bylaws with those in actual practice to prevent drift from the bylaws' original intentions.
Compensation	Reviews and approves compensation of board members and company executives.
Strategy	Reviews and approves company's strategic development plan.
Program Development	Reviews plans to address major problems and opportunities the company faces.

As you can gather from the list just described, the use of committees is a fluid situation. Depending on the board's needs, a committee can shift from ad hoc to a standing committee, such as the trend in recent years to make the audit function permanent. There are many such changes.

> Establishing too many committees dissipates the board's effectiveness and selection of the wrong committees or too few of them robs it of its most needed functions.

Taking Advantage of Advisory Councils

Richard was Chairman of the board and CEO of a small contract machining business in Michigan that he had built over the years into a mid-sized manufacturing firm supplying major automotive assembly plants. While other auto suppliers closed their doors during the last major recession, Richard's company held onto most of its customers by cutting costs and charging less for its products. Richard tells his story:

"As soon as car sales turned down we knew that in order to survive we had to cut costs and cut them dramatically so we could cut prices yet still squeeze out a profit.

Although we had several talented design and process engineers onboard and a local engineering consulting to draw talent from, we desperately needed help from professionals who could give us some perspective on the major steps we needed to take to survive. Things were that desperate.

A business friend of mine told me about advisory boards and some of the businesses their advice had helped improve. To make a long story short we tapped our contacts in companies across the USA and located some very gifted businesspeople who had advised companies in the metals manufacturing industry.

We formed an advisory council composed of some very bright senior executives from within and outside of the automotive business. The council eventually had a retired senior executive in the space vehicle manufacturing business, two top drawer fabrication engineering consultants, a management consultant who had helped design a well-known cost cutting program used by businesses throughout the country, a CPA, a cost accountant (and author of a popular book on cost accounting) and a couple of senior operating people from my company.

The council's strategic perspective gave us a blueprint to achieve our goal. Our engineers and engineering consultant and production people took it from there and designed some basic cost-cutting programs that saved the day. We owe much of our success to our advisory council that pointed the way."

Advisory councils come in many forms. The one described in the above example, created to help avoid a potential catastrophe, relies on the specific expertise of contributing members to resolve a major problem. Others, such as the CEO's special council includes fellow board chairmen or CEOs exclusively who bring to the table their combined years of experience as senior executives; men and women who have faced similar problems and can provide valuable insights.

Another type of advisory council works on legal and liability issues that confronts every board member in today's highly legalistic boardroom environment. A further example is a special events advisory board that brings together marketing, sales, advertising and promotional professionals to help smaller companies professionalize their sales and marketing efforts. There are many other such special purpose advisory councils.

Aaron Young, CEO of Laughlin Associates, a Nevada-based business services firm, discovered the value of an using an advisory council. "Recently, an advisor showed me the way to measure our website traffic against that of our competitors. I thought I knew about analytics, but in 15 minutes I learned more about that aspect of the business than I had in 10 years."[18]

Differences between Boards of Directors and Advisory Councils

Probably the biggest difference between boards of directors and advisory councils is that the latter has no fiduciary or legal standing while the former is regulated by law, is responsible to shareholders (the advisory council isn't) and in general has strict fiduciary and legal responsibilities.

Advisory boards have no power to direct the company's CEO and no power to either accept or reject recommendations on behalf of the company. Boards of directors, on the other hand, have the power to do all of those.

The board of directors of a company will be in existence for the life of the company, while an advisory council normally has a limited charter, which allows the CEO to dismiss the advisory board at will, change its direction entirely without acceptance by stockholders or replace its members whenever the CEO sees fit.

Normally members of the advisory council do not work as hard or contribute as much as board members, but of course that's also dependent on the type of advisory council. In the case of a company in trouble, such as in the example of Richard described a few pages before, advisory council members will put in the hours.

One of the distinct advantages of advisory councils is that members are not bound to political considerations and can speak their minds openly and honestly. That's quite often a huge advantage when board members are embroiled in political turf wars.

Another advantage of advisory councils is that they can attract professionals the company could not normally afford to hire. And, of course, the advisory council is free of the nightmare of lawsuits and has no need for the prohibitively expensive directors' and officers' liability insurance. And the fees companies pay for advisory board members (if any) come far below what board members receive for their work.

> Take advantage of advisory councils to help the company solve problems, seize market opportunities and improve company profitability.

SECTION FOUR

THE BOARD'S ROLE IN MERGERS AND ACQUISITIONS (M&A)

"We get talent and scale from mergers."

Angela Braly, Former President and Chief Executive Officer of WellPoint, Inc.

"When you have mergers and acquisitions that improve the quality of your product, the ability to grow and bring better efficiency, it's good for all."

Roger Agnelli, Founding partner and CEO of AGN Holding and TV commentator on business

"There is at least one point in the history of any company when you have to change dramatically to rise to the next level of performance. Miss that moment and you start to decline."

Andy Grove, Retired CEO of Intel Corporation and semiconductor industry pioneer

BOARD DUE DILIGENCE

Some70 percent to 90 percent of mergers and acquisitions fail. So the reality a CEO and his board of directors must face is that a successful merger or acquisition is never guaranteed, and the likelihood of failure is high. Cases in point: Sears & K-mart, Daimler Benz & Chrysler and AOL & Time Warner. Your fate in a merger or acquisition, however, doesn't have to lie in that direction. There are steps companies can take to recognize the complexity of the merger and acquisition (M&A) process facing them and go about their due diligence in such a way as to mitigate problems, both known and unknown.

The consultants of Bain & Company put it this way: "In the first decade of the century, M&A was an essential part of successful strategies for profitable growth. Many companies succeeded in delivering superior shareholder returns using M&A as a weapon for competitive advantage. *M&A strategy done right* (my emphasis), especially with a repeatable model built upon a disciplined M&A capability, creates value."[19]

The fact is that many high profile mergers and acquisitions have succeeded. For example, Disney-Pixar, Exxon-Mobil, and Sirius-XM. Bob Brauns, president of Marketplace Technologies agrees. "Most businesses grow 10, 15 or 20 percent per year," he explains. "If you're trying to achieve quantum jumps in growth, mergers and acquisitions is really the only way to do it."[20]

The point is that a merger or acquisition is of prime importance to a company's board of directors because either represents considerable risk and may substantially affect the company's future. Consequently, the board of directors must be involved in all decisions regarding M&A design and implementation.

Factors To Consider Before Merging or Acquiring a Company

Job candidates are trained to rehearse their "elevator pitch," a one to two minute summary of their backgrounds and qualifications. The elevator part refers to unexpectedly coming across a VIP in an elevator and pitching him for a job or referral. Of course, this rarely happens in real life. But it does happen when job candidates are pitching possible bosses in interviews, and that elevator pitch gets the ball rolling. It also speaks to the candidates' ability to succinctly describe what they can do for their companies.

The same kind of thinking applies to a merger or acquisition. If the Chairman of the board, CEO (or any board member) can't state in clear and unambiguous terms the value of a proposed merger or acquisition, and do so in about two minutes, the CEO will have trouble selling Wall Street analysts on its value. This acid test defines the ability of board members to think through every aspect of the proposed M&A.

Another way to look at the M&A elevator pitch is to ask these questions: "Why are we looking for a merger or acquisition? To increase market share? To buy a company with advanced technology? To enter a new market? Those kind of questions must be answered up front before your company begins the M&A election process. Once you have answered those questions, what follows is identification of target companies with the potential to significantly improve the combined company's value.

Assuming the board has already identified an M&A candidate and the potential for a substantial increase in valuation exists, the next step is to identify the key players on the M&A team both at your company and your potential partner's company as well as the third party go-between (if there is one) such as an investment bank or law firm. Getting to know the players involved is going to come in handy when you hit roadblocks . . . and you're going to hit roadblocks. The process is entirely too complicated to believe otherwise. Knowing whom to go to when you need to iron out problems may spell the difference between the parties reaching agreement or going their separate ways.

Know and understand goals of the company you intend to partner with, as well as their comparative place in their industry peer group (sales and profitability, ROI). The last thing you want, for instance, is a company that is gearing up to enter the low-price market when you're selling to the high-end of the market (unless you're interested in entering the low-price market). That kind of mistake is avoidable with just a little research.

And while you're in the investigative mode check the caliber of your proposed partner's senior executive team. If you don't have confidence in the integrity and competence of that team, move on to another company.

A football coach doesn't begin a game without a game plan. A general doesn't go into combat without an attack plan. What you're doing by attempting a merger or acquisition is a hundred-times more difficult. Your game or attack plan is called an M&A playbook (more on this in the next chapter). It will be your guiding document during the entire pre- and post-merger period. The inherent value of an M&A playbook is that it helps parties to the transaction think through every step of the process. You can bet that some of those companies whose mergers or acquisitions failed didn't take the time or put in the thought to develop an M&A playbook.

Study the market and competitive landscape to make sure the resulting merger or acquisition makes sense. If, for example, you expect more companies to enter your market, that will surely squeeze prices and profits, and the M&A venture may lose some of its luster. Don't ignore trends.

Walk away from any deal that doesn't meet your strategic goals, both financial and market-driven. If, for instance, your business model calls for you to be number one or number two in your market, and the merger or acquisition dilutes that expectation, abandon it. Instead seek merger or acquisition candidates in line with your business model.

As board members, do not allow senior operating executives to handle the merger or acquisition without oversight by the board . . . oversight that extends beyond a mere yes or no vote. Your obligation to the shareholders demands your full and complete understanding of what the merger or acquisition means to your company's future.

Evaluate cultural differences between partners. If your company has a regimented culture and your proposed partner has a laid back, laissez-faire culture, anticipate integration difficulties (unless you intend to operate both companies as separate entities).

Throughout the pre-and post-merger periods maintain a clear focus on customer requirements and how the merger or acquisition will affect quality and delivery of the goods and services they expect.

> Pay close attention to the Pre-M&A investigation. It lays the groundwork for a successful merger or acquisition.

Determining Synergy of the Deal and Whether It's Worthwhile

It's also known as 1 + 1 = 3, where the combined value of the two partners is greater than the separate value of each company. Will that happen? If it doesn't, the merger or acquisition may not be worthwhile. Post-merger share price must rise to reflect the value of the deal. Both parties to the transaction must feel they've gained or they'll never enter into the transaction to start with.

Determining whether the deal is worthwhile is a complex process because of the many variables that must be considered. Board members need to answer a host of questions surrounding any proposed merger or acquisition. For example:

Strategy Implications

1. Does the proposed merger or acquisition support the company's strategy?

2. Is it likely to have the support of shareholders?

3. Does the company have the necessary people, technical ability and financial resources to handle the merger or acquisition?

4. Does the company have the ability to handle any expected legal or regulatory requirements?

5. Is the merger or acquisition likely to be challenged by the government, and if so, what is the likely outcome?

6. Where will the resources to perform the due diligence come from? Are the people trained, and if not, how will they be trained and by whom?

Finance and Market Metrics

1. What financial effect will the merger or acquisition have on shareholder value? Will the rate of return improve and by how much?

2. Has EBITDA been analyzed, projected, and compared to other companies within the same industry? Will the merger or acquisition improve EBITDA and by how much and for how long?

3. How much will the company's valuation improve by?

4. Will the merger or acquisition place the company in a favorable financial position vis-à-vis competitors and peer group industry averages?

5. Will the company be able to keep its market prices competitive after the merger or acquisition?

6. What are the projected KPIs and does the merger or acquisition favorably affect them?

Integration Planning

1. Looking at the merger or acquisition from an overall standpoint, does it make sense? Does the combination of companies result in something with the potential for flourishing in today's demanding market economy?

2. Are the cultures of the two companies different? If so, how much, and does it make sense to bring them together or operate each as a separate company?

3. If the plans are to bring them together into one company, what steps will the company take to meld the cultures?

4. Are integration plans in place to assure as smooth as possible a transition?

5. What fallback plans does the company have in place if the merger or acquisition is not successful? And how is success defined?

6. What plans does the company have for assuring continuity of operations during the M&A transition process?

> Boardroom due diligence is the crucial first step in M&A planning. All pertinent questions need to be answered to the board's satisfaction before permitting a merger or acquisition to go forward.

THE M&A PLAYBOOK

According to Mike Myatt, chief strategy officer of N2Growth, "Most people tend to look at acquisitions from a rather myopic and traditional M&A perspective: making a strategic or synergistic purchase of an operating entity on an accretive basis. However restricting your view of acquisitions to operating companies is like playing a football game with only one play in your playbook. The truth is that acquisitions aren't just about buying companies, they're about value creation."[21]

Those are words to keep in mind. The entire M&A process is so long, so intricate and so involved it's easy to lose track of the original purpose—value creation. And that's the reason for the M&A playbook: to keep partnering companies in an M&A transaction on track, on time and focused on the end result of value creation through a series of instructions, guidelines, procedures, checklists and timetables.

Unfortunately, there is no one single M&A playbook template that companies considering mergers and acquisitions can use. Consequently, some M&A playbooks are short (relatively speaking), some long (a few even up to 1000 pages) , and all are germane only for the their specific companies. In other words, each M&A playbook has its own DNA.

Nevertheless, M&A playbooks share many common characteristics. Broadly speaking those include:

1. Transition planning

2. Company due diligence

3. Integration planning, and

4. Implementation

All M&A playbooks define the M&A process model to follow including specified deal strategy, governance practices, cultural integration, development of the appropriate metrics, timetables, contingency plans, checklists, expected synergies (valuation, sales, costs, quality, delivery time), and tax planning, identification of data rooms—to name the most prevalent. (Data rooms are secure rooms where information for the M&A of both companies are stored under lock and key and are accessible to specified parties only. The data room can be an actual locked room or it can be a restricted online website.)

Let's examine typical subject matter the M&A playbook will address.

Transition Planning

This first stage takes place early before consummation of the actual transaction. Bear in mind that the company will need to develop scalable processes tailor-made for the merger or acquisition. Since no two mergers or acquisitions are exactly the same, the playbook will have to be modified for each new merger or acquisition.

A key step is developing an M&A team that will analyze the company's ability to handle a merger or acquisition, including anticipated handicaps, coupled with identification of a path to proceed with the M&A transaction. This analysis will expose the most troublesome integration issues and suggest solutions.

This analytical phase drives the diagnostic stage where specific remedies emerge and M&A design starts, including preparation of the M&A playbook.

It helps at this stage to develop a strategy describing exactly what your company intends to accomplish with a merger or acquisition and then zero in on potential targets. The strategy should be a short document, normally one or two pages at most. Too many pages may diffuse the message.

When evaluating specific candidates consider such factors as value creation, costs and potential financial liabilities, management team capability, workplace culture and practices that could hinder a smooth integration.

This is the time to make a preliminary assessment of your potential partner's fit with your company and the relationship's viability. A more detailed assessment will follow later.

> A successful transition phase is key to developing a reliable and workable M&A playbook. Don't rush through it.

Company Due Diligence

Nothing is as unsettling as surprises in a potential merger or acquisition. That means that somebody or a group of somebodies haven't done their due diligence. Too much is riding on the outcome for each partner to have the merger or acquisition come apart because of flagrant errors, an important matter overlooked or lack of attention to important details.

This means accurately identifying important considerations such as costs, revenues, variances, unreported contracts and buried health care and retirement benefits.

It also means correctly reporting major problems or potential problems; for instance adverse market trends, anticipated labor disputes or loss of a major supplier or customer, any of which could substantially damage the company's profitability and share price.

Here are a few other items that require due diligence reporting, especially if there are anticipated disputes: intellectual property, patents, sales or market agreements with other companies, vital technologies and the technologists that operate them.

In general make sure to report thoroughly on all corporate records, operating and financial reports, business contracts, legal documents and procedures, ongoing or anticipated litigation, legal filings with state and federal government, tax liabilities, property owned (both physical and intellectual), employee records, insurance policies, and many other important records and transactions, of which there are simply too many to list here.

Most acquisitions involve acquiring customers as a major consideration. Customer due diligence should be done early and specifically. Way too often it is done last, because the seller does not want to upset its customers. And yet that is frequently the most important unrecorded asset to be acquired.

Deal structure should be considered early in the process. Whether it is an asset deal or a stock deal changes the valuation considerations. The earlier the better. All presumptions should be vetted, all unrecorded liabilities searched for.

> Most M&A deals that fall apart are traceable to a failure to perform proper due diligence. Assign your best detail people to handle this important task.

Integration Planning

This is a defining period,when planning the integration of the two companies occurs. It's also the time that if anything can go wrong it will. A successful integration plan depends on how well the board and company handled transition planning and conducted company due diligence.

The integration planning phrase is also a test of how well the board and company plans to conduct business as usual during the transition period. That task can be the hardest. Sales and operations must continue unabated. There can be no letup even when the merger or acquisition is taking place.

Human resources (HR) takes center stage. Employees may have new supervisors, new workplaces, new or modified work schedules and new leadership and legacy cultures. HR is tasked with the responsibility of assimilating new employees from one company into the next without disruption and keeping them motivated and productive. Moreover, HR is responsible for providing training for the combined workforce.

Operating managers have the difficult job of creating a new job structure, defining changed employee roles and training employees about unfamiliar operating procedures.

Customers of the combined venture will need to be assured that, from their perspective, it's business as usual and that they can expect a steady, uninterrupted supply of the goods and services the separate companies now provide.

Implementation

This is where it all comes together. It's when the company knows how good or poorly a job it did for all of the previous steps described in the M&A playbook. It's a time that exposes problems of almost any variety, ranging from inadequate employee indoctrination to a wide array of technical glitches that had not been foreseen. And it puts pressure on operating department heads to resolve those problems and glitches promptly. Assuming a smooth integration and implementation, they should be at a minimum.

The length of time and additional resources it takes to get the new company on track will be the true measure of how effective the merger or acquisition was.

> The conclusion of a merger or acquisition is a perfect time to sharpen and refine your M&A playbook for future mergers or acquisitions, based on your experience this time around.

Due Diligence Differences Between Selling the Business and Buying a Company

This is a good time to discuss some of the major differences regarding due diligence for selling a business and buying a company. It doesn't negate what you have just read, but it allows you to emphasize certain areas of due diligence over others depending on your perspective.

Selling A Business

This is not a matter of running an ad in The Wall Street Journal or Craigslist seeking buyers. That approach is more than likely telling the world that you desperately need to sell the business and you want to do it pronto. The last thing you want to do is scare potential buyers. A targeted campaign will attract buyers, not chase them away.

Hide nothing, disclose all. Those should be words that guide you throughout the transaction. If there is one word that resonates in an M&A—in fact in every business transaction—it's "integrity." Those who resort to trickery are soon mocked and shunted aside by businesspeople everywhere.

Consider opening negotiations with a floor and a ceiling price in mind. Know what bottom price you will absolutely insist on, and negotiate up to the ceiling. If the ceiling price is lower than, or in the range of, industry norms you stand a better chance of getting it.

Understand that buyers will check you out. And not only with a D&B report or an in-depth look at your business practices and financials, but also with people you have dealt with such as banks, suppliers and customers. If your reputation is sterling that will go a long way to convincing potentials buyers to start negotiating with you.

Along the same line, have your financial reports audited by a public accounting firm and the valuation of your company verified.

Buying a Company

Assess the value of the company's assets and liabilities, earnings, cash flow and working capital as well as future market and financial projections. Assure that the company's shares do not have restrictive covenants or liens attached to them.

Identify the company's major systems for both operations and financial control. If the seller is a manufacturing company, assess its quality program and such related factors as warranty costs, scrap and rework.

Review the management team in place along with the company's compensation policies and employment contracts.

Review the labor contract, if the company has one, and analyze if and how much the union presence hinders cost reduction and productivity improvement (always a consideration).

Evaluate the worth of the company's intellectual property including proprietary technical 'know-how,' blueprints, patents, written procedures and manuals among others.

Determine what contracts the company has in place and their value.

Search for unrecorded liabilities or issues; including potential tax issues, litigation issues, warranty issues or potential supply chain issues. Remember, at least half of your due diligence is searching for unrecorded potential problems.

SECTION FIVE

COUNTERING CYBER RISK

"U.S. computer networks and databases are under daily cyber attack by nation states, international crime organizations, sub-national groups, and individual hackers."

John O. Brennan, Director of the Central Intelligence Agency

"Hackers are breaking the systems for profit. Before, it was about intellectual curiosity and pursuit of knowledge and thrill, and now hacking is big business."

Kevin Mitnick, World's most famous hacker, now CEO of Mitnick Security Consulting, LLC

"Cyber bullies can hide behind a mask of anonymity online, and do not need direct physical access to their victims to do unimaginable harm."

Anna Maria Chavez, CEO, Girl Scouts of America

RISKS FROM NEW TECHNOLOGY

Bob, Chairman and CEO of a hospital supply company in the Northeast, and an enthusiastic user of new technology, was usually among the first in his industry to adopt advances on the cyber front.

His company had a web presence describing the company and its products, along with a sophisticated and secure online ordering system that customers could use to replenish hospital supplies. His production planning, inventory control and distribution systems were handled by the latest computer software, as was his operational and financial reporting.

Bob's company also had a presence on Facebook, LinkedIn, Twitter, Flickr, and he was experimenting with new social networks. He used them all to engage and communicate with his current customers and to attract new business. In many respects Bob's digital savvy was well ahead of the curve and it showed in excellent sales growth and increasing profitability and company ROI.

Furthermore, he was an enthusiastic supporter of advanced concepts such as mobility studies ("the set of people, processes and technology focused on managing the increasing array of mobile devices, wireless networks, and related services to enable broad use of mobile computing in a business context.[22]"), and 3D printing (producing physical goods such as clothing, car parts, houses, camera lenses, and body parts through special printers).

Bob was also a proponent of online data rooms and he established one when his company began the process of acquiring a smaller manufacturer of hospital supplies. This time, however, Bob wasn't so lucky. The data room was hacked by a business espionage thief and the contents sold to Bob's main competitor (or so Bob thought, because shortly after the theft, the competitor entered markets that mimicked Bob's strategy and plans with the same mix of products Bob's company sold), forcing Bob to cancel the acquisition.

Corporate Risk Management in An Age of Cyber Attacks

Increasingly, companies are becoming more susceptible to cyber attacks from many fronts besides desktop and laptop computers and smart phones. Day by day the ability of thieves to take advantage of technological breakthroughs is increasing.

Take 3D copiers (also called 3D printing or additive manufacturing) for example. This new technology has so many potential applications that a genuine concern is the production and sales of counterfeit products. The 3D copying process is so exact (variances less than the thickness of a human hair) it's virtually impossible to tell the difference between the original and counterfeit copies. This can present a huge problem for an acquiring company, and the board must take this factor into account. The black market for such counterfeit goods is enormous and highly profitable.

Then there is the garden variety of hacking, which to date had been wildly successful. Nextgov.com reports a staggering amount of daily cyber-incidents.[23] Here are three examples of the number of cyber-intrusion attempts recorded:

- British Petroleum: 50,000

- The Pentagon: 10,000,000

- The State of Michigan: 20,000,000

The Heritage Foundation claims " . . . the average cost of cyber crime for U.S. retail stores more than doubled from 2013 to an annual average of $8.6 million per company in 2014. The annual average cost per company of successful cyber attacks increased to $20.8 million in financial services, $14.5 million in the technology sector, and $12.7 million in communications industries.[24]"

The website Hackmageddon.com lists 18 hacking techniques clever cyber-thieves use, including malware, defacement, malicious iframe, ATM malware, Apache vulnerability, and DNS poisoning. The most frequent attacks were against industry, such as the hacking of millions of credit cards from Target, followed by government. [25]

Board members need to be aware of this surge of cyber attacks and the never-ending ingenuity of hackers to discover new and more devious ways to get information. They're rampant and ever increasing. A company's operational and financial reports are at risk as well as its intellectual property such as patents, engineering drawings, scientific formulas, contracts and other proprietary information. Criminals consider such targets virtual gold mines.

The Anti-Cyber Attack's Committee Charter

Elizabeth Bart writing in Millimam's website said, "Executive management and boards of directors need to think through the full range of cyber exposures and examine all contributing sources of cyber risk in designing what must be an integral component of an organization's enterprise risk management process.[26]"

Your company needs to form an anti-cyber-attack group composed of professionals from information technology, human resources, finance, corporate management and corporate security. The company CEO or president, with his chief financial officer at his side, should manage the group, and with strategic implications in mind, craft a policy and plan of action to combat cyber attacks.

The group's charter should have such elements as these:

- Investigate possible functions where cyber attacks can happen. This analysis should include not only where breaches have occurred, but also where they might happen. Determine the security of operational and financial systems, including their reports.

- Rate the ability of the company's internal controls and theft deterrence systems.

- Complete risk assessments for the functions just described and assess the probability risk for each to be compromised. Develop risk profiles.

- Ascertain the costs of implementing monitoring systems in vulnerable areas.

- Evaluate the capability of the company's IT team to thwart cyber attacks.

- Develop a security business model that recognizes the many organizational interrelationships needed to prevent cyber attacks and create policies and action plans listing assignments of what's to be done, by whom and under what conditions. This will include persons authorized to handle enterprise computers, cloud access, data rooms and related cyber-sensitive areas.

- Document processes involving security and make them specific enough and clear enough that employees will understand them, their purpose and the preventive steps described in the procedure.

- Develop analytics that accurately and timely reflect problems encountered, and apply statistically-based (3 Sigma) control charts to highlight functions in need of improvement.

- Consider board oversight essential. Board members can no longer consider the threat of cyber attack as something that happens to the other guy, the other company. It's pervasive, it's here now and it's dangerous.

Give the highest priority to your anti-cyber-attack group, publicize it widely across the company, and be sure to receive frequent reports for oversight purposes.

The Critical Importance of IT Leadership

Information technology is the cornerstone of security control for the prevention of and defense against cyber attacks. Sadly, studies of hacked companies have demonstrated that not all IT professionals are created equally. For example, many still have not changed the original security codes of their enterprise system computers, leaving them exposed to cyber attack. A company can have the best security systems in place but if it's stacked with outdated codes it nullifies the protection needed to stop hackers or saboteurs cold.

And that goes back to IT leadership. People who occupy this vital position in companies today need to exhibit the same leadership skills as leaders in other functions of the company, namely listening well and communicating clearly, being proactive, understanding how to motivate employees by establishing a collaborative workplace, being decisive and so forth. I don't think it's necessary to enumerate each of those characteristics because you're undoubtedly familiar with them.

Let's talk specifically about IT leadership characteristics in terms of cyber security. Elements would include:

- Aligning the IT function to serve company goals and establishing a framework within which IT is best able to support the company's strategy. Nowhere is this more important than in the realm of IT security.

- Educating employees about the dangers of cyber attacks and security breaches, and providing protocols and procedures that specify good security practices.

- Creating contingency plans in case of a successful cyber attack that provide specific duties and responsibilities for all involved employees from Chairman of the board through those charged with digital and systems responsibilities.

- Assuring that the most up-to-date anti-virus software is installed on all company computers, mobile devices, and that Wi-Fi networks are made invulnerable to attack.

- Practicing cyber attack simulations. Patterned on think tank war games, simulations prepare the company for real cyber attacks, so employees have some familiarity with defensive procedures in a real cyber emergency.

- Limiting specified employees to access of sensitive company data, and forbidding any new software, cyber procedures or anything else in the realm of cyber security to be changed, added or modified without first receiving permission from the IT director.

- Eliminating undue complexity. In Section One of this book a sub-heading titled How Esoteric and Overly-Sophisticated Plans Miss The Mark shows how overly complex information systems came close to shutting down a company. The smart and engaged information technology leader will never allow this to happen.

- Advances in technology are continuing to drive transformational change in every aspect of society. In the business world, while new technologies can spur greater productivity and efficiency, open new avenues to compete and accelerate growth, they also present new sources of risk, from privacy and security concerns to the sudden emergence of disruptive competitors. Directors need to know how technology trends are impacting their companies and boardrooms; what skills sets are needed to help rethink a company's approach to technology and to anticipate market trends in order to harness new opportunities and prepare for potential risks.

> Your company needs to pay as much attention to selection of an IT director or chief information officer as it does to any other senior executive.

APPENDIX

JOB DESCRIPTIONS

Sample Job Description of a Board Member Along With Some Recommendations

First, and most important, as a board member understand that you are held responsible for the company's success or failure. The decisions you make have serious consequences. Shareholders can lose substantial amounts of money, employees can lose jobs, the community within which the company operates can suffer. Knowing this unalterable fact, you also have the following duties and responsibilities to the company and yourself as explained below:

- Maximize shareholder value.

- Set an ethical tone for the company.

- Avoid conflicts of interest; subordinate your personal gain to the company's.

- Set the company's vision (or carry it on from the founder), and develop a strategy to achieve the vision.

- Assure the company has the resources and capacity to accomplish its strategy.

- Establish fiscal governance standards and assure the company has sound financial policies and practices.

- Oversee and assure compliance to legal and regulatory requirements.

- Approve the annual budget and large capital expenditures.

- Hire, mentor, evaluate and if necessary fire the CEO.

- Attract, recruit and retain board members.

- Approve the hiring, promotion and compensation packages of senior executives.

- Establish oversight mechanisms of company performance and identify variances to plan.

- Approve metrics that measure company performance.

- Evaluate, approve and oversee major changes that affect the company's future.

- Serve on committees as needed.

- Keep an arm's length from the operating departments. Don't get involved with making operating decisions.

- Recognize and prepare for threats to the company such as product recalls, major legal challenges and cyber attacks.

- Promote the company's image in the business and local community.

- Recognize that sooner or later you will be sued. Anticipate that all documentation will end up in court. Make sure you're covered in full for indemnity by the company and with a director's and officers' liability policy.

- Attend board meetings regularly and participate to the best of your ability. Know that if you don't you're furthering your risk of being sued for negligence.

- Be proactive. Instead of reacting to arising problems, anticipate them and prepare for their resolution before they get out of hand.

- Review the board agenda before meetings and prepare your contribution.

CONTACTING THE AUTHOR

Thank you for taking the time to read this book to prepare your board members and yourself for the rigors and rewards of serving on a board of directors. I know what you're experiencing because that's the business I'm in. It's been my privilege and my pleasure to serve on several boards of directors and consult with many other boards in the small to mid-cap market.

If you have any questions or comments about the book or any concern about your personal board service, please do not hesitate to contact me. In the meantime, best of luck.

4 Morningside Drive

Old Bridge, NJ, 08857-2714

Cell: 908-307-1113

krautwilliam9@gmail.com

LinkedIn: www.linkedin.com/in/billkraut

NOTES

1 This phrase was mentioned in Doug Tatum's book 'No Man's Land: Where Growing Companies Fail'.

2 SHRM website, President/CEO job description http://www.shrm.org/templatestools/samples/jobdescriptions/pages/cms_001618.aspx

3 Joel Trammel, *Lead From The Top:* Entrepreneur.com website, http://www.entrepreneur.com/article/233354, May 1, 2014

4 N2growth blog, *Managing the Board—Ten Things Every CEO Should Know,* Feb 14, 2012 http://www.n2growth.com/blog/managing-board-relations/

5 http://www.russellreynolds.com/content/essential-elements-effective-ceo-board-relationship

6 *Directors &Boards,* http://www.edelsontech.com/files/Problems_With_Boards_of_Small_Companies.pdf

7 A quote from The Honorable Myron T. Steele, Chief Justice, Delaware Supreme Court, http://www.nacdonline.org/education/? navItemNumber=510

8 Edward L. Cochran, Managing Abnormal Situations in the Process Industries: Automation, People, Culture, Honeywell Technology Center

9 Gurdeep Mahal ,A Complex Quality Management System Doesn't Mean It's Effective, Quality Digest, 12/03/2013

10 John Reh, About Money, An Interview with Leslie Kossof on Management Leadership Skills, http://management.about.com/od/leadership/a/LKdrea m01.htm

11 *Competitive Strategy* (1986). Michael Porter. Harvard Business School Press

12 http://www.entrepreneurship.org/resource-center/exit-strategies.aspx

13 Scott Keller, Michiel Kruyt and Judy Malan, How Do I Develop An Effective Top Team?, McKinsey & Company's Insight Into Organization

14 Mary Genis, So Many leadership Programs, So Little Change, Effective Approaches to Leadership Development, *Journal for Non Profit Management*, 2008

15 From article titled "Be Brutally Efficient", INC ., September, 2014, page 78.

16 Kevin Sharer, How Should Your Leaders Behave, *Harvard Business Review*, Oct, 2013

17 Josh Linkner, 7 Tips to Run Better Board Meetings, *Forbes Online*, June 28, 2013, http://www.forbes.com/sites/joshlinkner/2013/06/28/7-tips-to-run-better-board-meetings/

18 Randy Myers, Collective Wisdom, *INC,* Nov, 2014, page 60

19 *Acquisition Strategy,* Bain & Company, http://www.bain.com/consulting-services/mergers-and-acquisitions/acquisitions-strategy.aspx

20 Bob Brauns, M&A Mania: Is It Right for Your Company? http://www.va-interactive.com/inbusiness/editorial/finance/articles/manda.html

21 Mike Myatt, M@A Without Buying the Company, Creative Acquisitions, N2Growth blog, http://www.n2growth.com/blog/ma-without-buying-the-company/#sthash.1ifjJT4l.dpuf

22 Wikipedia

23 How Many Cyber attacks Hit The United States Last Year?, Nextgov.com http://www.nextgov.com/cybersecurity/2013/03/how-many-cyberattacks-hit-united-states-last-year/61775/

24 Riley Waters, Cyber Attacks on US Companies in 2014, *The Heritage Foundation* blog, Oct 27, 2014, http://www.heritage.org/research/reports/2014/10/cyber-attacks-on-us-companies-in-2014

25 October 2014 Cyber Attacks Statistics, Hackmageddon.com, http://hackmageddon.com/category/security/cyber-attacks-statistics/

26 Elizabeth Bart, Cyber Risk Management: Breaches, Threats, and Vulnerabilities, *Milliman*, Dec 24, 2012 http://us.milliman.com/insight/pc/Cyber-risk-management-Breaches--threats--and-vulnerabilities/#